HOUSEHOLD HINTS

**TIPS TO REMEDY
THIS OR THAT IN THE HOUSEHOLD.**

Copyright © 1998 Rada Mfg. Co.

All rights reserved. No part of this work may be reproduced in any manner without prior written permission of the publisher, Rada Mfg. Co. Credit to publisher must be included in any excerpt.

Printed in the United States
ISBN 1-56383-081-7

Item #8200

TABLE OF CONTENTS

I. QUICK COOKING REFERENCES 1

- Common Kitchen Pans and Volumes 1
- Quantities To Serve 100 People 4
- Substitutions 6
- Oven Temperatures 12
- Deep-Fat Frying, Temperatures 12
- Simplified Measures 13
- Equivalents for Common Cooking Ingredients ... 14
- Contents of Cans 15
- Common Cause Of Failure In Baking 16
- What To Use Spices And Seasonings For 21
- Food Guide Pyramid 25

II. FOOD HINTS AND HELPS 26

- Apples 26
- Barbecues 29
- Berries 32
- Breads 35
- Breakfast 39
- Cakes And Frostings 41
- Cookies 45
- Eggs 50
- Nuts 55
- Pickling And Preserving 57
- Pies 60
- Salads 64
- Vegetables 68
- Miscellaneous 77

III. HOUSEHOLD INFORMATION 110
- Windows 110
- Furniture 112
- Laundry 121
- Bathroom 126
- Handy Person 131
- Beauty 136
- Sewing 141

IV. FOOD STORAGE... 144
WHAT TO KEEP, HOW TO KEEP IT AND HOW LONG TO KEEP IT

V. TO REMOVE STAINS FROM WASHABLES 152

VI. 99 WAYS YOU CAN SAVE THE EARTH 170

VII. PLANT INFORMATION 187

I. QUICK COOKING REFERENCES

COMMON KITCHEN PANS TO USE WHEN THE RECIPE CALLS FOR:

4-CUP BAKING DISH:

9-inch pie plate

8 x 1 1/4-inch layer cake pan - C

7 3/8 x 3 5/8 x 2 1/4-inch loaf pan - A

6-CUP BAKING DISH:

8 or 9 x 11 1/2-inch layer-cake pan - C

10-inch pie plate

8 1/2 x 3 5/8 x 2 5/8-inch loaf pan - A

8-CUP BAKING DISH:

8 x 8 x 2-inch square pan - D

11 x 7 x 1 1/2-inch baking pan

9 x 5 x 3-inch loaf pan - A

10-CUP BAKING DISH:

9 x 9 x 2-inch square pan - D

11 3/4 x 7 1/2 x 1 3/4-inch baking pan

15 x 10 x 1-inch jellyroll pan

12-CUP BAKING DISH OR OVER:

12 1/3 x 8 1/2 x 2-inch glass baking pan	12 cups
13 x 9 x 2-inch metal baking pan	15 cups
14 x 10 1/2 x 2 1/2-inch roasting pan	19 cups

G

H

I

J

K

TOTAL VOLUME OF VARIOUS SPECIAL BAKING PANS

Tube Pans:
7 1/2 x 3-inch "Bundt" tube - K	6 cups
9 x 3 1/2-inch fancy tube or "Bundt" pan - J or K	9 cups
9 x 3 1/2-inch angel cake pan - I	12 cups
10 x 3 3/4-inch "Bundt" or "Crownburst" pan - K	12 cups
9 x 3 1/2-inch fancy tube - J	12 cups
10 x 4-inch fancy tube mold (kugelhupf) - J	16 cups
10 x 4-inch angel cake pan - I	18 cups

Melon Mold:
7 x 5 1/2 x 4-inch mold pan - B	6 cups

Spring-Form Pans:
8 x 3-inch pan - B	12 cups
9 x 3-inch pan - B	16 cups

Ring Mold:
8 1/2 x 2 1/4-inch mold - E	4 1/2 cups
9 1/4 x 2 3/4-inch mold - E	8 cups

Charlotte Mold:
6 x 4 1/4-inch mold - G	7 1/2 cups

Brioche Pan:
9 1/2 x 3 1/4-inch pan - F	8 cups

QUANTITIES TO SERVE 100 PEOPLE

Coffee	3 lbs.
Cream	3 qts.
Whipping cream	4 pts.
Milk	6 gallons
Fruit cocktail	2 1/2 gallons
Fruit juice	4 #10 cans
Tomato juice	4 #10 cans
Soup	5 gallons
Hot Dogs	25 lbs.
Meat loaf	18 to 22 lbs.
Ham	40 lbs.
Beef	40 lbs.
Roast pork	40 lbs.
Hamburger	30 to 36 lbs.
Chicken for chicken pie	40 lbs.
Potatoes	35 lbs.
Scalloped potatoes	4 gals.
Spaghetti	5 gals.
Vegetables	4 #10 cans
Baked beans	5 gals.
Beets	25 lbs.
Cauliflower	18 lbs.
Cabbage for slaw	16 lbs.
Carrots	24 lbs.

Corn	2 #10 cans
Bread	10 loaves
Rolls	200
Butter	3 lbs.
Potato salad	3 1/2 to 4 gals.
Fruit salad	20 qts.
Vegetable salad	20 qts.
Lettuce	16 lg. heads
Salad dressing	3 qts.
Jello	2 1/2 qts.
Pies	18
Cakes	8
Ice Cream	4 gallons
Cheese	3 lbs.
Olives	1 3/4 lbs.
Pickles	2 qts.
Nuts	3 lbs.

To serve 50 people, divide by 2. To serve 25 people, divide by 4.
Cooking for a crowd. The season of the year rules the food choices to a degree. Also variety in flavor, texture, color and form. Plan best use of refrigerator space. Decide type of service, buffet, family style or served plates with waitresses.

SUBSTITUTIONS

FOR:	YOU CAN USE:
1 T. cornstarch	2 T. flour OR 1 1/2 T. quick cooking tapioca
1 C. cake flour	1 C. less 2 T. all-purpose flour
1 C. all-purpose flour	1 C. plus 2 T. cake flour
1 square chocolate	3 T. cocoa and 1 T. fat
1 C. melted shortening	1 C. salad oil (may not be substituted for solid shortening
1 C. milk	1/2 C. evaporated milk and 1/2 C water
1 C. sour milk or buttermilk	1 T. lemon juice or vinegar and enough sweet milk to measure 1 C.
1 C. heavy cream	2/3 C. milk and 1/3 C. butter
1 C. heavy cream, whipped	2/3 C. well-chilled evaporated milk, whipped
Sweetened condensed milk	No substitution

1 egg	2 T. dried whole egg and 2 T. water
1 tsp. baking powder	1/4 tsp. baking soda and 1 tsp. cream of tartar OR 1/4 tsp. baking soda and 1/2 C. sour milk, buttermilk or molasses; reduce other liquid 1/2 C.
1 C. sugar	1 C. honey; reduce other liquid 1/4 C.; reduce baking temperature 25°
1 C. miniature marshmallows	About 10 large marshmallows, cut up
1 medium onion (2 1/2" dia.)	2 T. instant minced onion OR 1 tsp. onion powder OR 2 tsp. onion salt; reduce salt 1 tsp.
1 garlic clove	1/8 tsp. garlic powder OR 1/4 tsp. garlic salt, reduce salt 1/8 tsp.
1 T. fresh herbs	1 tsp. dried herbs OR 1/4 tsp. powdered herbs OR 1/2 tsp. herb salt; reduce salt 1/4 tsp.

SUBSTITUTIONS

For bread crumbs:
Use crushed corn or wheat flakes, or other dry cereal. Or use potato flakes.

For butter:
Use 7/8 cup of solid shortening plus 1/2 teaspoon of salt.

For fresh milk:
To substitute 1 cup of fresh milk, use 1/2 cup each of evaporated milk and water. For 1 cup of whole milk, prepare 1 liquid cup of nonfat dry milk and 2 1/2 teaspoons butter or margarine.

For sugar:
Use brown sugar, although it will result in a slight molasses flavor.

For superfine sugar:
Process regular granulated sugar in your blender.

For red and green sweet pepper:
Use canned pimientos.

For vanilla extract:
Use grated lemon or orange rind for flavoring instead. Or try a little cinnamon or nutmeg.

For flour:
Use 1 tablespoon cornstarch instead of 2 tablespoons of flour. Or try using instant potatoes or cornmeal.

For buttermilk:
Use 1 tablespoon of lemon juice or vinegar and enough fresh milk to make 1 cup. Let it stand 5 minutes before using.

For catsup:
Use a cup of tomato sauce added to 1 1/4 cups of brown sugar, 2 tablespoons of vinegar, 1/4 teaspoon of cinnamon and a dash of ground cloves and allspice.

For unsweetened chocolate:
Use 1 tablespoon of shortening plus 3 tablespoons of unsweetened chocolate to equal 1 square of unsweetened chocolate.

For corn syrup:
Use 1/4 cup of water or other type of liquid called for in the recipe, plus 1 cup of sugar.

For eggs:
Add 3 or 4 extra tablespoons of liquid called for in the recipe. Or, when you're 1 egg shy for a recipe that calls for many, substitute 1 teaspoon of cornstarch.

For cake flour:
Use 7/8 cup of all-purpose flour for each cup of cake flour called for in a recipe.

For fresh herbs and spices:
For 1/3 the amount of dried herbs or spices. Dried herbs are more concentrated.

For honey:
To substitute 1 cup of honey, use 1 1/4 cups of sugar and 1/4 cup of water or other liquid called for in the recipe.

OVEN TEMPERATURES

Slow	300°
Slow moderate	325°
Moderate	350°
Quick moderate	375°
Moderately hot	400°
Hot	425°
Very Hot	475°

DEEP-FAT FRYING TEMPERATURES WITHOUT A THERMOMETER

A 1-inch cube of white bread will turn golden brown:

345° to 355°	65 seconds
355° to 365°	60 seconds
365° to 375°	50 seconds
375° to 385°	40 seconds
385° to 395°	20 seconds

SIMPLIFIED MEASURES

Measure	Equivalent
1 tablespoon	3 teaspoons
2 tablespoons	1 ounce
1 jigger	1 1/2 ounces
1/4 cup	4 tablespoons
1/3 cup	5 tablespoons plus 1 teaspoon
1/2 cup	8 tablespoons
1 cup	16 tablespoons
1 pint	2 cups
1 quart	4 cups
1 gallon	4 quarts
1 liter	4 cups plus 3 tablespoons
1 ounce (dry)	2 tablespoons
1 pound	16 ounces
2.21 pounds	35.3 ounces

EQUIVALENTS FOR COMMON COOKING INGREDIENTS

1 lb.	**Apples**	3 or 4 medium
1 lb.	**Bananas**	3 or 4 medium
1 lb.	**Beans, dried**	5 to 6 cups cooked
1 quart	**Berries**	3 1/2 cups
1 slice	**Bread**	1/2 cup crumbs
1/4 lb.	**Cheese, grated**	1 cup
1 oz.	**Chocolate, 1 square**	1 T. melted
1/2 pint	**Cream**	1 cup
1 cup	**Cream, heavy**	2 cups whipped
1 lb.	**Flour, all-purpose**	4 cups sifted
1 envelope	**Gelatin**	1 T.
1 tsp.	**Herbs, dried**	1 T. fresh
2-3 T. juice	**Lemon**	1 1/2 tsp. grated rind
1 cup dry	**Macaroni**	2 1/4 cups cooked
1 lb.	**Meat, diced**	2 cups
1 lb.	**Mushrooms**	5-6 cups sliced
1/4 lb.	**Nuts, shelled**	1 cup chopped

CONTENTS OF CANS

Of the different sizes of cans used by commercial canners, the most common are:

Size	Average Contents
8 ounces	1 cup
picnic	1 1/4 cups
No. 300	1 3/4 cups
No. 1 tall	2 cups
No. 303	2 cups
No. 2	2 1/2 cups

COMMON CAUSES OF FAILURE IN BAKING

BISCUITS

1. Rough biscuits caused from in sufficient mixing.

2. Dry biscuits caused from baking in too slow an oven and handling too much.

3. Uneven browning caused from cooking in dark surface pan (use a cookie sheet or shallow bright finish pan), too high a temperature and rolling the dough too thin.

MUFFINS

1. Coarse texture caused from insufficient stirring and cooking at too low a temperature.

2. Tunnels in muffins, peaks in center and soggy texture are caused from overmixing.

3. For a nice muffin, mix well but light and bake at correct temperature.

CAKES

1. Cracks and uneven surface may be caused by too much flour, too hot an oven and sometimes from cold oven start.

2. Cake is dry may be caused by too much flour, too little shortening, too much baking powder or cooking at too low a temperature.

3. A heavy cake means too much sugar has been used or baked too short a period.

4. A sticky crust is caused by too much sugar.

5. Coarse grained cake may be caused by too little mixing, too much fat, too much baking powder, using fat too soft, and baking at too low a temperature.

6. Cakes fall may be caused by using insufficient flour, under baking, too much sugar, too much fat or not enough baking powder.

7. Uneven browning may be caused from cooking cakes at too high a temperature, crowding the shelf (allow at least 2" around pans) or using dark pans (use bright finish, smooth bottomed pans).

8. Cake has uneven color is caused from not mixing well. Mix thoroughly, but do not over mix.

PIES

1. Pastry crumbles caused by overmixing flour and fat.

2. Pastry is tough caused by using too much water and over mixing dough.

3. Pies do not burn - for fruit or custard pies use a Pyrex pie pan or an enamel pan and bake at 400° to 425° constant temperature.

BREADS (YEAST)

1. Yeast bread is porous - this is caused by over-rising or cooking at too low a temperature.

2. Crust is dark and blisters - this is caused by over-rising, the bread will blister just under the crust.

3. Bread does not rise - this is caused from over-kneading or from using old yeast.

4. Bread is streaked - this is caused from underkneading and not kneading evenly.

5. Bread baked uneven - caused by using old dark pans, too much dough in pan, crowding the oven shelf or cooking at too high temperature.

WHAT TO USE SPICES & SEASONINGS FOR:

ALLSPICE: Cakes, cookies, pies, breads, puddings, fruit preserves, pickles, relishes, yellow vegetables.

BASIL: Tomatoes, tomato sauce, barbecue sauce, salads.

CLOVES: Ham, beets, pickling, beef marinades, hot spiced beverages, cakes, pies, puddings.

DILL: Salads and salad dressings, sour cream or mayonnaise dips, eggs, cucumbers, tomatoes, carrots, fish, cheese dishes.

CELERY SEED: Meat loaf; beef, lamb and vegetable stews; bean salad.

CHILI POWDER: Vegetable and beef chili, cocktail and barbecue sauces, egg dishes, meatballs, meat loaf.

CINNAMON: Cakes, cookies, pies, puddings, coffee, dessert topping, yellow vegetables, hot spiced beverages.

GARLIC: Nearly all types of meat, fish, poultry, vegetables, sauces, stews, soups, salads and salad dressings.

OREGANO: Tomatoes, tomato sauce, green vegetables, salads and salad dressings, beef, poultry, seafood, eggs, marinades.

HORSERADISH: Cocktail sauce, sour cream dips, ham, sausage, boiled beef, smoked fish, salad dressings.

MARJORAM: Bread, veal, lamb, seafood, fowl, green vegetables, potatoes, tomatoes.

NUTMEG: Cakes, cookies, pies, puddings, eggnog, custards, creamed vegetables, stewed fruits, bean soups, poultry.

ROSEMARY: Lamb, poultry stuffing, beef and pork roasts, tomato sauce, salads, seafood, turnips, potatoes, cauliflower.

SAGE: Veal, sausage, poultry, stuffings, cheese spreads, soups.

TARRAGON: Salad dressings, sauces, egg dishes, stews, poultry, seafood.

THYME: Chowder, seafood, stuffing, poultry, meat, vegetables.

FOOD GUIDE PYRAMID

A Guide to Daily Food Choices

II. FOOD HINTS AND HELPS

WHICH APPLES ARE BEST?

BAKING: Albermarle Pippin, Granny Smith, Jonathan, Rome Beauty

EATING: Red And Yellow Delicious, Grimes Golden, Rome Beauty

PIE: Granny Smith, Grimes Golden, Rome Beauty, Stayman, Winesap

SALAD: Granny Smith, Grimes Golden, Red Delicious, Rome Beauty, York Imperial, Winesap

SAUCE: Early Harvest, Summer Rambo, Grimes Golden, Stayman, Winesap, York Imperial

APPLES

Place apple cider in 32 cup percolator coffeemaker and fill coffee basket 1/2 full of red-hot candies. Makes tasty spicy pink cider.

Premeasure and freeze apple slices for Apple Crisp recipes.

Substitute apples for blueberries in muffins.

Put 2 tablespoons apple juice concentrate in cream cheese frosting for applesauce cupcakes.

Keep apples from absorbing strong refrigerator odors by storing them in a plastic bag. They will stay fresher longer and won't speed ripening of other produce.

Toss lemon juice on cut-up apples to prevent browning.

Add 1/2 cup extra apples to a pie that you wish "very full".

Cut apple in half horizontally. Cut design in apple halves and use for stamps to decorate. Kids love this!

BARBECUES

It's simple to grill acorn squash. Pierce the skin with fork a couple of times, then wrap in aluminum foil. Grill over direct heat for 1 hour turning once. Remove from grill.

Venison or turkey burgers will not stick to grill when they are coated with nonstick cooking spray.

For tender flavorful spareribs begin by parboiling them in pineapple juice. Then add a homemade barbecue sauce while grilling.

Leftover barbecued pork chops make great sandwiches. Just remove meat from bones, reheat and serve on buns.

Here's an easy marinade for grilled pork chops; for four chops, combine 1/2 cup each soy sauce, water and honey. Pour over chops and marinate, leave covered in the refrigerator overnight. Grill until done as desired.

For fast, easy cleanup of food stuck inside pans, boil a little vinegar and water in the pan before washing. No scrubbing is required–the pan practically wipes clean.

Instead of taking time to make meatballs make "meat squares". Spread meat mixture in jelly roll pan and bake over coals or in oven. Cut in small squares.

To roast corn, pull back husks and remove silks. Replace husks and tie at top. Soak in salt water for 1 hour. Grill over hot coals for 15 to 20 minutes turning frequently.

Presoak bamboo skewers in water for 20 minutes before threading with meat, veggies or fruit to prevent them from scorching or burning.

Store already made hamburger patties on tray between waxed paper. Can lift for accessibility once grilling starts.

Old baking pans (even garage sale finds) clean up easily after grilling if they are completely covered with aluminum foil first. Once the cooking is done just remove foil and discard.

BERRIES

Using a potato blender is quicker than using a fork for mashing strawberries.

Berries will keep up to a week refrigerated unwashed and unsweetened in a loosely covered container.

When picking strawberries look under the leaves for the best berries as they will hide there.

Thawed frozen berries will always be softer and juicier than fresh berries. Defrost the sealed bag of frozen berries in a larger bowl of cold water for 10 to 15 minutes, then use them in recipes where the extra juice is a bonus, such as over shortcake or in a sauce for pound cake.

Strawberries can be used in punches as a garnish, in the ice ring itself, or as the base for a delicious punch. The berries can be mashed, strained to eliminate the seeds and doctored up as per recipe or imagination.

Premeasure berries, rhubarb, etc. for future baking projects in amounts called for in favorite recipes. Prevents messy measuring later.

Best way to pick berries is to pinch and twist the stems, leaving the hulls intact.

Remove stem and hull from fresh strawberries with a tomato corer.

Use sliced or mashed strawberries sprinkled with sugar for shortcake. If they stand for 20 to 30 minutes they will make their juice.

Use whole strawberries with pointed ends facing upward if you plan to glaze recipe.

Use egg slicer for cutting perfect slices of strawberries.

Strawberries are best if picked red and firm, but may be ripened if left on counter for a day.

For shortcake or scones use a rich hot fudge strawberry filling with one cup warmed hot topping and one cup sliced strawberries.

BREADS

Always brush the tops of your yeast breads and rolls with melted butter when you put the dough into the pans, but do it before it raises a final time. Use just enough butter to glaze the top. This adds flavor and brown color. Brush tops again with soft butter.

Add butterscotch chips to batter of pumpkin quick bread instead of raisins. More delicious!

Shredded green tomatoes may be substituted for zucchini in a zucchini bread recipe.

Homemade bread contains no preservatives and needs refrigeration. Bread that sounds hollow when tapped with fingers is baked perfectly.

Dough rises better if kept out of drafts. Cover with towel and set over a pilot light on stove (if you have one). Let dough "rest" before rolling it out to shape it—it will be less elastic and easier to handle.

Turn your basic recipe for 2 or 3 loaves of whole wheat bread into one for herb bread by adding 1/4 teaspoon each of marjoram, thyme, oregano and garlic powder and 1 tablespoon grated onion. Mix into the warm water or milk before adding the flour.

BREAKFAST

Keep bacon slices from sticking together; heat a spatula over a burner, slide it under each slice to separate it from others.

Use egg slicer to slice Kiwi uniformly.

For a perfect fried egg, put a little butter, bacon grease, or side pork fat into a skillet (cast iron is best). If you want it sunny-side up, put a cover on and the steam will take care of the egg. If you want it over easy, flip the egg over, and count to five slowly. Leave it longer if you like the yolks hard.

For crispy French toast, add a touch of cornstarch to the egg mixture.

To butter many slices of bread quickly and evenly, heat the butter until soft. Then use a pastry brush to paint the butter on.

For fluffier omelettes, add a pinch of cornstarch before beating.

To ripen Kiwi's, place them in a brown paper bag with a banana or apple and leave at room temperature. When they are ready to eat, they should yield to slight pressure. Store ripe fruit in refrigerator for up to one week.

To make an inexpensive syrup for pancakes, save small amounts of leftover jams and jellies in a jar. Or, fruit-flavored syrup can be made by adding 2 cups sugar to 1 cup of any kind of fruit juice and cooking until it boils.

Freeze waffles that are left; they can be reheated in the toaster.

CAKES AND FROSTINGS

When testing cake for doneness the rack may be pulled out a little only as it needs to stay close to the heat. Test with either toothpick or touch lightly with fingertips. If the cake bounces back it is done, if it leaves a dent, then it's not.

To keep a cake from sliding on its plate during transit, drizzle a bit of frosting in a circle on the plate where the cake will rest before removing the cake from the pan. The frosting will hold the cake in place.

Don't tamper with the mix or change it. If it says cream it means cream. If it says 2% then it means 2%.

Sweeten whipped cream with confectioners' sugar instead of granulated sugar. It will stay fluffy and hold up a lot longer.

Always let a cake cool 10 minutes before running a knife around the edge and turning out on a plate. An upside-down cake or jelly roll has to be removed at once.

Spray measuring spoons or cups with a coating of nonstick cooking spray before measuring honey, syrup, or molasses. Sticky ingredients slide right out with no mess.

If it calls for sour milk, and you have none, put 1 tablespoon of vinegar in one cup of milk, it will curdle immediately.

Be sure your rack is in the center of the oven or the cake will come out too brown either on the top or bottom.

If you are getting lopsided cakes then level up your stove.

To prevent icing from running off your cake, try dusting the surface lightly with cornstarch before icing.

Always refrigerate cream cheese-based frostings and fillings.

If you forget to preheat the oven, turn the broiler on for a minute to get the temperature up fast.

To dress up a plain frosted cake but have no sprinkles—crush sweetened cereal and scatter across the top. Adds a fun look and a nice crunch, too.

When it says to grease pan, it means only the bottom as the cake has to have something to hold on to.

To prepare muffins or cupcakes easily mix the batter in a pitcher so it can be poured in cups without making a mess.

To improve an inexpensive cake mix, add one tablespoon of butter to the batter. This will make a richer-tasting cake.

Try a little cream of tartar in your 7 minute icing, it will not get dry and cracked.

Shortly before taking cupcakes from the oven, place a marshmallow on each for quick frosting.

In place of flour use one teaspoon of tapioca for thickening in fruit pies.

COOKIES

Flour the rolling pin slightly and roll lightly to desired thickness. Cut shapes close together and keep all trimmings for the last.
Place pans in upper 1/3 of oven. Watch cookies carefully while baking to avoid burning edges.

Use only stick butter or margarine in these recipes. Don't use reduced-fat or tub products. The fat and moisture content will yield poor results.

For best results, bake one sheet of cookies at a time on the center rack \of your oven. You can bake two sheets—halfway through baking, switch the pans from one rack to the other.

Use outline (not solid) cookie cutters for napkins rings when having a party or country setting.

Use electric knife to slice rolled-chilled cookie dough.

For accuracy, measure liquids in clear measuring cups with spouts and hold the cup to eye level.

Add 1/2 cup of sour cream to your peanut butter cookie recipe to make your cookies more moist.

Lay a dampened cloth on your table or countertop before putting the cookie sheet down so it won't slide around while you fill it.

Most cookies can be stored at room temperature for a few days without losing flavor. For longer storage, place cookies and wax paper in layers in airtight container and freeze for 3 months.

For chewy cookies, bake until edges are golden and the center looks slightly underbaked. Cool on baking sheets for 1 to 2 minutes before removing to a wire rack.

When sprinkling sugar on cookies, try putting it into a salt shaker, as it saves time.

Beat butter and sugar at medium speed. Beat dry ingredients at low speed. Don't overbeat. The dough should be just blended.

Use nesting metal cups and spoons to measure flour and other dry ingredients. Before measuring, stir flour in its canister or package to aerate, then spoon it into appropriate-size measuring cup. Level off any excess with a metal spatula.

Cookie dough that is to be rolled is much easier to handle after it has been in a cold place for 10 to 30 minutes. This keeps it from sticking, even though it may be soft. If not done, the dough may require more flour and too much flour makes the cookies hard and brittle. In rolling, take out on a floured board only as much dough as can be managed easily.

Stale angel food cake can be cut into 1/2" slices and shaped with cookie cutters to make delicious "cookies". Just toast in the oven for a few minutes.

EGGS

If you shake the egg and you hear a rattle, you can be sure it's stale. A really fresh egg will sink and a stale one will float.

If you are making deviled eggs and want to slice it perfectly, dip the knife in water first. The slice will be smooth with no yolk sticking to the knife.

The white of an egg is easiest to beat when it's at room temperature. So leave it out of the refrigerator about a half an hour before using it.

To make light and fluffy scrambled eggs, add a little water while beating the eggs.

Add vinegar to the water while boiling eggs. Vinegar helps to seal the egg, since it acts on the calcium in the shell.

STORING EGGS: 1. Place your eggs in those tight-sealing egg containers and they will last longer in the refrigerator. You really shouldn't keep eggs longer than 11 days 2. Cover them with oil on the top in a sealed container in the refrigerator. 3. For long term storage: if there's a special on eggs at your local supermarket, you can take advantage of it. Just crack all the eggs open and put them in the freezer unit. To use one egg at a time, put single eggs in the ice tray. When frozen, put the egg cubes in a sealed plastic bag. You can take out the cubes one at a time for daily use. If you use eggs in twos or threes, freeze them that way in a plastic bag.

To make quick-diced eggs, take your potato masher and go to work on a boiled egg.

If you wrap each egg in aluminum foil before boiling it, the shell won't crack when it's boiling.

To make those eggs go further when making scrambled eggs for a crowd, add a pinch of baking powder and 2 teaspoons of water per egg.

A great trick for peeling eggs the easy way. When they are finished boiling, turn off the heat and just let them sit in the pan with the lid on for about 5 minutes. Steam will build up under the shell and they will just fall away.

Or, quickly rinse hot hard-boiled eggs in cold water, and the shells will be easier to remove.

Fresh or hard-boiled? Spin the egg. If it wobbles, it is raw - if it spins easily, it's hard boiled.

Add a few drops of vinegar to the water when poaching an egg to keep it from running all over the pan.

Add 1 tablespoon of water per egg white to increase the quantity of beaten egg white when making meringue.

Fresh eggs are rough and chalky in appearance. Old eggs are smooth and shiny.

Pierce the end of an egg with a pin, and it will not break when placed in boiling water.

Beaten egg whites will be more stable if you add 1 teaspoon cream of tartar to each cup of egg whites (7 or 8 eggs).

A small funnel is handy for separating egg whites from yolks. Open the egg over the funnel and the white will run through and the yolk will remain.

For baking, it's best to use medium to large eggs. Extra large may cause cakes to fall when cooled.

Brown and white shells are the same quantity.

Egg whites can be kept up to 1 year. Add them to a plastic container as you "collect them" for use in meringues, angel food cake...1 cup equals 7 or 8 egg whites. You can also refreeze defrosted egg whites.

For fluffier omelets, add a pinch of cornstarch before beating.

NUTS

Use English walnuts and Black Walnut extract as a substitute for Black Walnuts.

Cut nut bars into festive shapes for fun and variety at Holiday time.

Freeze nuts in shells a few days before cracking. The nutmeats will come out in larger pieces if they are frozen.

Make holiday treat of 1 1/2 lbs. white, dark or milk chocolate and one can of mixed nuts. Drop teaspoonfuls onto waxed paper to harden. Store in airtight container.

Before chopping nuts in a food processor, dust them with flour. This keeps the nuts from sticking to the processor.

Toasted almonds will chop easier than untoasted ones.

Shake chopped nuts in flour before adding to cake batter. This prevents them from sinking to the bottom.

Use a blender for quick coarsely chopped almonds.

Pecans stay fresh in refrigerator for 9 months and in freezer for 2 years.

Wear rubber gloves when husking Black Walnuts to prevent stains to the hands.

To quickly crack a large amount of nuts, put in a bag and gently hammer until they are cracked open. Then remove nutmeats with a pick.

If nuts are stale, place them in the oven at 250°F and leave them there for 5 or 10 minutes. The heat will revive them.

PICKLING AND PRESERVING

Quart jars are usually used for canning fruits, vegetables, meats and pickles. Pint jars are used for jams, preserves, relishes and sauces. Half-pint or jelly glasses are used for jams, jellies, butters and marmalades. The size of the family is important when choosing jar size.

Pressure canning means to be done in a pressure cooker. Leave an inch space between jars after they have been taken out of the boiling water for air to circulate between the jars.

Pickles and relishes can be eaten right away, but do get a better flavor the longer you wait. Dill pickles must wait 2 weeks.

Use heavy stainless steel kettles when possible. Never cook vinegar in cheap aluminum as it will take on the taste.

The number of jars you will get out of a recipe will vary because of the difference in the size and the moisture in the fruits and vegetables.

For all canned pickles, relishes, and vegetables do not use iodized salt or the ingredients will get mushy.

Syrups for jams and jellies will rise to top quickly and have to be watched very carefully.

Spices may be added to pickles or relishes as are or may be tied up in a clean cloth, cooked with the pickles and discarded when cooking is done before jars are filled.

When filling jars always clean the tops off from spills.

Never sit hot jars in a draft.

When they are cooling you will hear a popping if you are using the two-piece lids. That popping means what the jar has sealed. Press your finger on top; and if the cover is flat, it's okay. If jar has not sealed, use the contents—do not store.

To scald your jars means to sterilize your empty jars by standing them upright in boiling water and filling with more boiling water and boil a minute or two.

Sure-Jell helps set and speed-up jams and jellies but they can be cooked down low without it. Always ladle foam off of jams and jellies with a metal spoon.

PIES

Insert a knife into the slits of a double-crusted pie, and it should come out clear. If it is sugary it needs more baking.

Try not to make meringue on a humid day, since the sugar absorbs moisture and excess moisture may cause beading. Also be certain the sugar is completely dissolved during beating. Rub a small amount between your fingers-if it's grainy, continue to beat. Place the meringue over the hot filling. Keep filling warm while preparing meringue, pour it into the pie shell just before topping with meringue. Bake immediately at 350° for 15 minutes.

Spread meringue so it extends out to the edge of the crust so it won't pull away. It's sealed.

Add 1 or 2 tablespoons of molasses to pumpkin pie filling. It will make it richer in color and tastier, too.

Use a thimble to cut holes in your top pie crusts. Then replace cut-out circles back in their holes. The hole will get bigger as pie bakes, giving an interesting pattern.

If recipe calls for milk, use whole milk. Store-bought does not have as much butterfat as farm milk, but it is just fine.

No matter how much salt a recipe calls for—put it in there as it is there for a reason.

Make nice fat pies and heap the filling into the crusts.

Place your pastry-lined pie plate on a partially pulled-out oven rack, then carefully fill with mixture. Gently push rack in stove.

Place a piece of plastic wrap over cooked custard or pudding after pouring into pie shell to prevent a "skin" from forming.

Add one tablespoon sesame seeds to pie crusts recipe to have a tasty nutty flavor.

Be sure your rolling pin is wood and heavy enough. Some are too light. A medium pin weighs about 5 lbs. and is fine.

If a recipe calls for a cup, don't put in a rounded cup. Unless it says "heaping", use only a level measure.

When measuring shortening for pie crust wet the cup first, and the shortening will slide right out.

Where a recipe calls for 2 cups freshly whipped cream, use 12 ounces of Cool Whip.

SALADS

Green peppers will not last long in the refrigerator. The best way to have them available is to freeze them. Wash them after hollowing out the insides, dry them and put them in a plastic bag. You can dice, strip, cube, or chip them.

Iceberg lettuce as well as escarole and spinach is used for a bed for small and large salads, of any kind.

The classic salad of iceberg lettuce is always welcome to the American table. It is used along with dressings or mixed with a variety of dark greens. It can be eaten dressed up very little or dressed up a lot with a variety of fruits, vegetables, meats, etc.

Salads are light or complex and are usually chosen according to the meal they are served with. Fresh, tart greens will balance a heavy meal. A complex salad containing many ingredients will complement a lighter meal.

Potato salads, a Waldorf salad, bean and mayo-dressed salads are generally informal, good picnic fare and healthy.

Buffet salads are spreads with eye-appeal. They are molds, filled vegetable containers, marinated vegetables, and decoratively garnished salad platters.

A basic earthy salad is nothing more than the edible parts of herbs and plants, gently seasoned with the most basic of spices or a sprinkling of lemon juice or vinegar and oil.

Optimal freshness is the hallmark of a successful salad.

Most salads should be served at room temperature.

Flowers such as roses, daylillies, nasturtiums, geraniums and marigolds are commonly used in salads. They bruise easily so must be gotten early in the morning and handled carefully.

Kale, beet greens, Swiss chard, bok choy, and the cabbages—including red, green and napa, and savory are all great additions to any salad, adding flavor and texture.

To keep mint, lemon verbena, etc. from taking over your herb garden, pull your needed amounts by the roots. Enough root will remain for the plants to continue growing.

Just about any cut of meat, fowl, or fish can be worked into a salad. Such salads can often be served as the main course.

Remove all fat and gristle when preparing meat. Cut meat across the grain into even thickness strips. Arrange slices in a neat, decorative pattern on a platter.

Place unripened tomatoes with other fruit, especially pears to speed up ripening.

Commercial or homemade dressings are a matter of choice.

VEGETABLES

To save potatoes before sprouting– peel, slice and boil them partially. Drain, cool and freeze. When needed pop frozen potatoes into boiling water, finish cooking and then mash.

Use an egg slicer to slice mushrooms perfectly.

Use an ice cream scoop to remove seeds from acorn or Hubbard squash or even pumpkin seeds from pumpkins.

Freeze your onion surplus. Slice or dice and bake in a covered casserole at 350° until they're tender, about 20 to 30 minutes. Cool and pack them in freezer containers in recipe-sized portions. Freeze for up to 6 months. To use, thaw and warm with a little butter until light golden brown–perfect for casseroles, burgers or in gravies.

When cutting corn from the cob to freeze, place end of cob in the hole of a Bundt pan. Cut corn off with sharp knife and corn will fall right in pan with little mess.

One pound of fresh spinach will yield 10 to 12 cups of torn leaves; which will cook down to about one cup.

Put foil under sweet potatoes before baking so sticky juices can't mess up oven.

Use nylon stocking to dry onions. Put one in toe, tie a knot, put in onion, tie a knot-continue to stocking top. Hang in dry place. When needed cut one off between knots.

Substitute lemon pepper seasoning for table salt.

Cook equal amounts of potatoes and turnips in boiling salted water until tender. Mash with milk and butter. Real treat!

To preserve garden fresh carrots, dig from ground, wash well, dry overnight, pack in plastic bags and store in refrigerator and enjoy all winter.

For a quick scalloped potato, combine frozen French fries with a homemade cheese sauce and bake until bubbly.

Bake a potato casserole right along with your roast.

Chickens that are fed large cucumbers will produce eggs larger in size and quantity.

For the fluffiest mashed potatoes, use only russets and be careful not to overbeat. Cook just until tender; immediately drain and let stand uncovered for 1 to 2 minutes. While beating, slowly add warm milk. Do not add butter.

If fresh vegetables are wilted or blemished, pick off the brown edges. Sprinkle with cool water, wrap in towel and refrigerate for an hour or so.

Perk up soggy lettuce by adding lemon juice to a bowl of cold water and soak for an hour in the refrigerator.

Lettuce and celery will crisp up fast if you place it in a pan of cold water and add a few sliced potatoes.

If vegetables are overdone, put the pot in a pan of cold water. Let it stand from 15 minutes to 1/2 hour without scraping pan.

By lining the crisper section of your refrigerator with newspaper and wrapping vegetables with it, moisture will be absorbed and your vegetables will stay fresher longer.

Store leftover corn, peas, green beans, carrots, celery, potatoes and onions in a container in the freezer. Add to other ingredients when making stew.

To keep the flavor in the vegetables, add a small amount of sugar to the water after cooking carrots, peas, beets, and corn.

Onions, broccoli and Brussels sprouts will cook faster if you make an X-shaped cut at the base of the vegetable.

Overcooked potatoes can become soggy when the milk is added. Sprinkle with dry powdered milk for the fluffiest mashed potatoes ever.

To hurry up baked potatoes, boil in salted water for 10 minutes, then place in a very hot oven. Or, cut potatoes in half and place them face down on a baking sheet in the oven to make the baking time shorter.

Save some of the water in which the potatoes were boiled - add to some powdered milk and use when mashing. This restores some of the nutrients that were lost in the cooking process.

Use a couple of tablespoons of cream cheese in place of butter for your potatoes; try using sour cream instead of milk when mashing.

To avoid tears when peeling onions, peel them under cold water or refrigerate before chopping.

For sandwiches to go in lunchboxes, sprinkle with dried onion. They will have turned into crisp pieces by lunchtime.

Keep tomatoes in storage with stems pointed downward and they will retain their freshness longer.

Sunlight doesn't ripen tomatoes. It's the warmth that makes them ripen. So find a warm spot near the stove or dishwasher where they can get a little heat.

Save the juice from canned tomatoes in ice cube trays. When frozen, store in plastic bags in freezer for cooking use or for tomato drinks.

Put vegetables in water after the water boils - not before - to be sure to preserve all the vegetables' vitamins.

Squash that is leftover can be improved by adding some maple syrup before reheated.

When cooking dried beans, add salt after cooking; if salt is added at the start, it will slow the cooking process.

Adding sugar and horseradish to cooked carrots improves the flavor.

MISCELLANEOUS

SYRUP

For each cup of light syrup in a recipe, substitute one cup of sugar and 1/4 cup water. For each cup of dark corn syrup, substitute 1 cup packed brown sugar and 1/4 cup water.

TREAT FOR SAUERKRAUT

To have a tangy combination add a can of whole-berry cranberry sauce to your package of sauerkraut as it's heating plus a little brown sugar. A real treat!

FROZEN CONCENTRATE

To use frozen concentrate to prepare juice quickly, slide it into a pitcher, add some water and mash with a potato masher. Will be a lot quicker and dissolves readily.

GRATED LEMON PEEL
The quickest way to make grated lemon peel for recipes is to slice off big pieces of peel and grind them for just a few seconds in a food processor.

HOT CHOCOLATE
To prevent "skin" from forming on top of hot chocolate beverages, beat hot cocoa with whisk until foamy.

STRINGING POPCORN
If you plan to string popcorn, pop the popcorn a few days ahead. The kernels will not break as bad when needle is pushed through.

ICE WATER
Fill a clean plastic milk jug half full of water and freeze. When ice water is needed just finish filling with water and take along on a picnic, etc.

BROWN SUGAR
A little brown sugar will help flavor chili.

MEATLOAF
Put meatloaf ingredients in a bowl and mix with a potato masher to prevent a mess, especially on your hands.

DECORATIVE POTATO OR MACARONI SALAD
For a decorative potato or macaroni salad, dissolve a little unflavored gelatin in a small amount of water and mix with the mayonnaise before adding to the salad. Spread the salad in a mold and chill. When turned out the salad will keep its shape.

TENDER PANCAKES OR WAFFLES
For light and tender pancakes or waffles, separate the egg and beat the white until stiff. Stir the yolk and other liquid ingredients into the dry ingredients, then fold in the beaten egg white.

VENISON
Cook venison in slow cooker. Add a tad of the apple pie spice and black pepper to cut the wild flavor.

CANDLES
Before having a party or decorating with candles, put candles in the freezer for a few hours. They will not drip wax then.

SALT
If stew is too salty, add raw cut potatoes and discard once they have cooked and absorbed the salt. Another remedy is to add a teaspoon each of cider vinegar and sugar. Or, simply add sugar.

If soup or stew is too sweet, add salt. For a main dish or vegetable, add a teaspoon of cider vinegar.

GRAVY
To make gravy smooth, keep a jar with a mixture of equal parts of flour and cornstarch. Put 3 or 4 tablespoons of this mixture in another jar and add some water. Shake, and in a few minutes you will have a smooth paste for gravy.

To remedy greasy gravy, add a small amount of baking soda.

For quick thickener for gravies, add some instant potatoes to your gravy and it will thicken beautifully.

Pour a cup of brewed coffee around a roast or turkey as you put it in the oven. The dark savory gravy is always perfect.

Add a few teaspoons of soy sauce to gravies and stews for a great flavor and color.

A QUICK WAY TO WHIP CREAM
A pinch of salt added to the cream before whipping strengthens the fat cells and makes them more elastic. This helps the cream stiffen much more quickly.

CREAM THAT WILL NOT WHIP

Chill cream, bowl and beater well. Set bowl of cream into a bowl of ice water while you're whipping. Add the white of an egg. Chill and then whip. If the cream still does not stiffen, gradually whip in 3 or 4 drops of lemon juice. Cream whipped ahead of time will not separate if you add a touch of unflavored gelatin (1/4 teaspoon per cup of cream). To eliminate a lot of mess when whipping cream with an electric beater, try this: Cut 2 holes in the middle of a piece of waxed paper, then slip the stems of the beaters through the holes and attach the beaters to the machine. Simply place paper and beaters over the bowl and whip away.

ROCK-HARD BROWN SUGAR
Add a slice of soft bread to the package of brown sugar, close the bag tightly, and in a few hours the sugar will be soft again. If you need it in a hurry, simply grate the amount called for with a hand grater. Or, put brown sugar and a cup of water (do not add to the sugar, set it alongside of it) in a covered pan. Place in the oven (low heat) for a while. Or, buy liquid brown sugar.

CAKED OR CLOGGED SALT
Tightly wrap a piece of aluminum foil around the salt shaker. This will keep the dampness out of the salt. To prevent clogging, keep 5 to 10 grains of rice inside your shaker.

NO SPATTERING OR STICKING
To keep frying food from spattering, invert a metal colander over the pan, allowing steam to escape.

Always heat the frying pan before adding oil or butter. This will keep things from sticking to the pan.

Boil vinegar in a brand new frying pan to keep things from sticking to it.

HURRY-UP HAMBURGERS
Poke a hole in the middle of the patties while shaping them. The burgers will cook faster and the holes will disappear when done.

SHRINKLESS LINKS
Boil sausage links for about 8 minutes before frying and they will shrink less and not break at all. Or, you can roll them lightly in flour before frying.

REMOVING THE CORN SILK
Dampen a paper towel or terry cloth and brush downward on the cob of corn. Every strand should come off.

PREVENTING BOIL-OVERS
Add a lump of butter or a few teaspoons of cooking oil to the water. Rice, noodles or spaghetti will not boil over or stick together.

SOFTENING BUTTER
Soften butter quickly by grating it. Or heat a small pan and place it upside-down over the butter dish for several minutes. Or place in the microwave for a few seconds.

MEASURING STICKY LIQUIDS
Before measuring honey or syrup, oil the cup with cooking oil and rinse in hot water.

SCALDED MILK
Add a bit of sugar (without stirring) to milk to prevent it from scorching.

Rinse the pan with cold water before scalding milk, and it will be much easier to clean.

TENDERIZED MEAT
Boiled meat: Add a tablespoon of vinegar to the cooking water.

Tough meat or game: Make a marinade of equal parts cooking vinegar and heated bouillon. Marinate for 2 hours.

Steak: Simply rub in a mixture of cooking vinegar and oil. Allow to stand for 2 hours.

Chicken: To stew an old hen, soak it in vinegar for several hours before cooking. It will taste like a spring chicken.

UNPLEASANT COOKING ODORS
While cooking vegetables that give off unpleasant odors, simmer a small pan of vinegar on top of the stove. Or, add vinegar to the cooking water. To remove the odor of fish from cooking and serving implements, rinse in vinegar water.

CLEAN AND DEODORIZE YOUR CUTTING BOARD
Bleach it clean with lemon juice. Take away strong odors like onion with baking soda. Just rub it in.

KEEP THE COLOR IN BEETS
If you find that your beets tend to lose color when you boil them, add a little lemon juice.

NO-SMELL CABBAGE
Two things to do to keep cabbage smell from filling the kitchen: don't overcook it (keep it crisp) and put half a lemon in the water when you boil it.

A GREAT ENERGY SAVER
When you're near the end of the baking time, turn the oven off and keep the door closed. The heat will stay the same long enough to finish baking your cake or pie and you'll save all that energy.

GRATING CHEESE
Chill the cheese before grating and it will take much less time.

SPECIAL LOOKING PIES
Give a unique look to your pies by using pinking shears to cut the dough. Make a pinked lattice crust!

REMOVING HAM RIND
Before placing ham in the roasting pan, slit rind lengthwise on the underside. The rind will peel away as the ham cooks, and can be easily removed.

UNMOLDING GELATIN
Rinse the mold pan in cold water and coat with salad oil. The oil will give the gelatin a nice luster and it will easily fall out of the mold.

NO-SPILL CUPCAKES
An ice cream scoop can be used to fill cupcake papers without spilling.

SLICING CAKE OR TORTE
Use dental floss to slice evenly and cleanly through a cake or torte - simply stretch a length of the floss taut and press down through the cake.

ICE CREAM
Buy bulk quantities of ice cream and pack in small margarine containers. These provide individual servings.

CANNING PEACHES
Don't bother to remove skins when canning or freezing peaches. They will taste better and be more nutritious with the skin on.

HOW TO CHOP GARLIC
Chop in a small amount of salt to prevent pieces from sticking to the knife or chopped board. Then pulverize with the tip of the knife.

EXCESS FAT ON SOUPS OR STEWS
Remove fat from stews or soups by refrigerating and eliminating fat as it rises and hardens on the surface. Or add lettuce leaves to the pot - the fat will cling to them. Discard lettuce before serving.

BROILED MEAT DRIPPINGS
Place a piece of bread under the rack on which you are broiling meat. Not only will this absorb the dripping fat, but it will reduce the chance of the fat catching on fire.

FAKE SOUR CREAM
To cut down on calories, run cottage cheese through the blender. It can be flavored with chives, extracts, etc., and used in place of mayonnaise.

BROWNED BUTTER
Browning brings out the flavor of the butter, so only half as much is needed for seasoning vegetables if it is browned before it is added.

FRESH GARLIC
Peel garlic and store in a covered jar of vegetable oil. The garlic will stay fresh and the oil will be nicely flavored for salad dressings.

FLUFFY RICE
Rice will be fluffier and whiter if you add 1 teaspoon of lemon juice to each quart of water.

NUTRITIOUS RICE
Cook rice in liquid saved from cooking vegetables to add flavor and nutrition. A nutty taste can be achieved by adding wheat germ to the rice.

PERFECT NOODLES
When cooking noodles, bring required amount of water to a boil, add noodles, turn heat off and allow to stand for 20 minutes. This prevents overboiling and the chore of stirring. Noodles won't stick to the pan with this method.

EASY CROUTONS
Make delicious croutons for soup or salad by saving toast, cutting into cubes, and sautéing in garlic butter.

BAKED FISH
To keep fish from sticking to the pan, bake on a bed of chopped onion, celery and parsley. This also adds a nice flavor to the fish.

NON-STICKING BACON
Roll a package of bacon into a tube before opening. This will loosen the slices and keep them from sticking together.

TASTY HOT DOGS
Boil hot dogs in sweet pickle juice and a little water for a different taste.

GOLDEN-BROWN CHICKEN
For golden-brown fried chicken, roll it in powdered milk instead of flour.

DOUBLE BOILER HINT
Toss a few marbles in the bottom of a double boiler. When the water boils down the noise will let you know!

FLOUR PUFF
Keep a powder puff in your flour container to easily dust your rolling pin or pastry board.

JAR LABELS
Attach canning labels to the lids instead of the sides of jelly jars, to prevent the chore of removing the labels when the contents are gone.

DIFFERENT MEATBALLS
Try using crushed cornflakes or corn bread instead of bread crumbs in a meatball recipe. Or use onion-flavored potato chips.

CLEAN-UP TIPS

APPLIANCES
To shine chrome, use vinegar or window cleaner.

If the numbers on your oven dial are worn, take a yellow crayon and rub it all over the number on the dial. Gently wipe off the excess crayon and paint with the clear nail polish.

To clean splattered food from the interior of your microwave, bring one cup of water to a boil until steam forms on the inside walls of microwave. Remove water and wipe with a damp cloth. You may have to repeat the process to get a really big job done.

To rid yellowing from white appliances try this: Mix together: 1/2 cup bleach, 1/4 cup baking soda and 4 cups warm water. Apply with a sponge and let set for 10 minutes. Rinse and dry thoroughly.

Instead of using commercial waxes, shine with rubbing alcohol.

For quick clean-ups, rub with equal parts of water and household ammonia.

Or, try club soda. It cleans and polishes at the same time.

BLENDER
Fill part way with hot water and add a drop of detergent. Cover and turn it on for a few seconds. Rinse and drain dry.

COPPER POTS
Fill a spray bottle with vinegar and add 3 tablespoons of salt. Spray solution liberally on copper pot. Let set for a while, then simply rub clean. Dip lemon halves in salt and rub. Or, rub with Worcestershire sauce or catsup.

The tarnish will disappear. Clean with toothpaste and rinse.

BURNT AND SCORCHED PANS
Sprinkle burnt pans liberally with baking soda, adding just enough water to moisten. Let stand for several hours. You can generally lift the burned portions right out of the pan.

Stubborn stains on non-stick cookware can be removed by boiling 2 tablespoons of baking soda, 1/2 cup vinegar and 1 cup water for 10 minutes. Re-season pan with salad oil.

CAST-IRON SKILLETS
Clean the outside of the pan with commercial oven cleaner. Let set for 2 hours and the accumulated black stains can be removed with vinegar and water.

CAN OPENER
Loosen grime by brushing with an old toothbrush. To thoroughly clean blades, run a paper towel through the cutting process.

ENAMELWARE OR CASSEROLE DISHES
Fill a dish that contains stuck food bits with boiling water and 2 tablespoons of baking soda. Let it stand and wash out.

DISHES
Save time and money by using the cheapest brand of dishwashing detergent available, but add a few tablespoons of vinegar to the dishwater. The vinegar will cut the grease and leave your dishes sparkling clean.

Before washing fine china and crystal, place a towel on the bottom of the sink to act as a cushion.

To remove coffee or tea stains and cigarette burns from fine china. Rub with a damp cloth dipped in baking soda.

DISHWASHER
Run a cup of white vinegar through the entire cycle in an empty dishwasher to remove all soap film.

CLOGGED DRAINS
When a drain is clogged with grease, pour a cup of salt and a cup of baking soda into the drain followed by a kettle of boiling water. The grease will usually dissolve immediately and open the drain.

Coffee grounds are a no-no. They do a nice job of clogging, especially if they get mixed with grease.

CURTAINS
To freshen curtains, throw in the dryer with a fabric softener sheet and a damp towel.

COBWEBS
To remove cobwebs, clean with an upward motion to lift them off. Downward motions tend to splatter them against walls.

DUSTING
Spray furniture polish on the bristles of your broom and the dust and dirt will be easier to collect when you sweep.

DISH DRAINER
Remove hard water stains from your dish drainer by tilting the low end of the board slightly and pouring one cup of white vinegar over the board. Let it set overnight and rub off with a sponge in the morning.

GARBAGE DISPOSAL
Grind a half lemon or orange rind in the disposal to remove any unpleasant odor.

GLASSWARE
Never put a delicate glass in hot water bottom side first; it will crack from sudden expansion.

The most delicate glassware will be safe if it is slipped in edgewise. Vinegar is a must when washing crystal. Rinse in 1 part vinegar to 3 parts warm water. Air dry.

When one glass is tucked inside another, do not force them apart. Fill the top glass with cold water and dip the lower one in hot water. They will come apart without breaking.

GRATER
For a fast and simple clean-up, rub salad oil on the grater before using.

Use a toothbrush to brush lemon rind, cheese, onion or whatever out of the grater before washing it.

MEAT GRINDER
Before washing, run a piece of bread through it.

OVEN
Following a spill, sprinkle with salt immediately. When oven is cool, brush off burnt food and wipe with a damp sponge.

Sprinkle bottom of oven with automatic dishwasher soap and cover with wet paper towels. Let stand for a few hours.

A quick way to clean oven parts is to place a bath towel in the bathtub and pile all removable parts from the oven onto it. Draw enough hot water to just cover the parts and sprinkle a cup of dishwasher soap over it. While you are cleaning the inside of the oven, the rest will be cleaning itself.

An inexpensive oven cleaner: Set oven on warm for about 20 minutes, then turn off. Place a small dish of full strength ammonia on the top shelf. Put a large pan of boiling water on the bottom shelf and let it set overnight. In the morning, open oven and let it air a while before washing off with soap and water. Even the hard baked-on grease will wash off easily.

PLASTIC CUPS, DISHES AND CONTAINERS
Coffee or tea stains can be scoured with baking soda.

Or, fill the stained cup with hot water and drop in a few denture cleanser tablets. Let soak for 1 hour.

To rid foul odors from plastic containers, place crumpled-up newspaper (black and white only) into the container. Cover tightly and leave overnight.

REFRIGERATOR
To help eliminate odors fill a small bowl with charcoal (the kind used for potted plants) and place it on a shelf in the refrigerator. It absorbs odors rapidly.

An open box of baking soda will absorb food odors for at least a month or two.

A little vanilla poured on a piece of cotton and placed in the refrigerator will eliminate odors.

To prevent mildew from forming, wipe with vinegar. The acid effectively kills the mildew fungus.

Use a glycerine soaked cloth to wipe sides and shelves. Future spills wipe up easily. And after the freezer has been defrosted, coat the inside coils with glycerin. The next time you defrost, the ice will loosen quickly and drop off in sheets.

Wash inside and out with a mixture of 3 tablespoons of baking soda in a quart of warm water.

SINKS

For a sparkling white sink, place paper towels across the bottom of your sink and saturate with household bleach. Let set for 1/2 hour or so.

Rub stainless steel sinks with lighter fluid if rust marks appear. After the rust disappears wipe with your regular kitchen cleanser.

Use a cloth dampened with rubbing alcohol to remove water spots from stainless steel.

Spots on stainless steel can also be removed with white vinegar.

Club soda will shine up stainless steel sinks in a jiffy.

TEA KETTLE
To remove lime deposits, fill with equal parts of vinegar and water. Bring to a boil and allow to stand overnight.

THERMOS BOTTLE
Fill the bottle with warm water, add 1 teaspoon of baking soda and allow to soak.

TIN PIE PANS
Remove rust by dipping a raw potato in cleaning powder and scouring.

TO UNPLUG SINK
Pour in one cup or more of white vinegar and a cup of baking soda, then add hot water out of the tap at full force. When bubbling stops, drain should be clear. Need no plumber.

FINGERPRINTS OFF THE KITCHEN DOOR AND WALLS
Take away fingerprints and grime with a solution of half water and half ammonia. Put in a spray bottle from one of these expensive cleaning products, you'll never have to buy them again.

FORMICA TOPS
Polish them to a sparkle with club soda.

SILVER
Clean with toothbrush.

III. HOUSEHOLD INFORMATION

WINDOWS

WINDOW CLEANING
Newspaper is much cheaper to use for drying freshly-washed windows than paper toweling.

DRYING WINDOWS
Dry the inside panes with up-and-down strokes, and the outside with back-and-forth motions to see which side has smudges.

WINDOW CLEANING SOLUTION
The best mixture for cleaning windows is 1/2 cup of ammonia, 1 cup of white vinegar and 2 tablespoons of cornstarch in a bucket of warm water.

COLD WEATHER WINDOW CLEANING
Add 1/2 cup of rubbing alcohol to the above mixture on cold days to prevent ice from forming on your windows.

CLEAN WINDOW SILLS
To remove spots on window sills, rub the surface with rubbing alcohol.

ALUMINUM WINDOW FRAMES
Use cream silver polish to clean aluminum window frames.

GREASE SPOTS
Any cola drink will remove grease spots from windows.

NUMBERED WINDOWS
When cleaning, painting or changing windows, number each with a ballpoint pen and put the corresponding number inside the proper window frame.

WINDOW SHADE TEARS
Repair with colorless nail polish. This works wonders on small tears.

CLEANING SCREENS
For a thorough job, brush on both sides with kerosene. Wipe with a clean cloth. This method will also prevent rust from forming. Be sure to dust the screens with a small paintbrush before you begin.

For small jobs, rub a brush-type hair roller lightly over the screen and see how easily it picks up all the lint and dust.

FURNITURE

TO REMOVE POLISH BUILD-UP
Mix 1/2 cup vinegar and 1/2 cup water. Rub with a soft cloth that has been moistened with solution, but wrung out. Dry immediately with another soft cloth.

POLISHING CARVED FURNITURE
Dip an old soft toothbrush into furniture polish and brush lightly.

CIGARETTE BURNS
For small minor burns, try rubbing mayonnaise into the burn. Let set for a while before wiping off with a soft cloth.

Burns can be repaired with a wax stick (available in all colors at paint and hardware stores). Gently scrape away the charred finish. Heat a knife blade and melt the shellac stick against the heated blade. Smooth over damaged area with your finger. But always consider the value of the furniture. It might be better to have a professional make the repair.

Or, make a paste of rottenstone (available at hardware stores) and salad oil. Rub into the burned spot only, following the grain of wood. Wipe clean with a cloth that has been dampened in oil. Wipe dry and apply your favorite furniture polish.

SCRATCHES
Make sure you always rub with the grain of the wood when repairing a scratch.

Walnut:
Remove the meat from a fresh, unsalted walnut or pecan nut. Break it in half and rub the scratch with the broken side of the nut.

Mahogany:
You can either rub the scratch with a dark brown crayon or buff with brown paste wax.

Red Mahogany:
Apply ordinary iodine with a number 0 artist's brush.

Maple:
Combine equal amounts of iodine and denatured alcohol. Apply with a Q-tip, then dry, wax and buff.

Ebony:
Use black shoe polish, black eyebrow pencil or black crayon.

Teakwood:
Rub very gently with 0000 steel wool. Rub in equal amounts of linseed oil and turpentine.

Light-finished furniture:
Scratches can be hidden by using tan shoe polish. However, only on shiny finishes.

For all minor scratches:
Cover each scratch with a generous amount of white petroleum jelly. Allow it to remain on for 24 hours. Rub into wood. Remove excess and polish as usual.

For larger scratchers:
Fill by rubbing with a wax stick (available in all colors at your hardware or paint store) or a crayon that matches the finish of the wood.

REMOVING PAPER THAT IS STUCK TO A WOOD SURFACE
Do not scrape with a knife. Pour any salad oil, a few drops at a time, on the paper. Let set for a while and rub with a soft cloth. Repeat the procedure until the paper is completely gone.

Old decals can be removed easily by painting them with several coats of white vinegar. Give the vinegar time to soak in, then gently scrape off.

THREE SOLUTIONS TO REMOVE WHITE WATER RINGS AND SPOTS
Dampen a soft cloth with water and put a dab of toothpaste on it. For stubborn stains, add baking soda to the toothpaste.

Make a paste of butter or mayonnaise and cigarette ashes. Apply to spot and buff away.

Apply a paste of salad oil and salt. Let stand briefly. Wipe and polish.

MARBLE TABLE-TOP STAINS
Sprinkle salt on a fresh-cut lemon. Rub very lightly over stain. Do not rub hard or you will ruin the polished surface. Wash off with soap and water.

Scour with a water and baking soda paste. Let stand for a few minutes before rinsing with warm water.

REMOVING CANDLE WAX FROM WOODEN FINISHES
Soften the wax with a hair dryer. Remove wax with paper toweling and wash down with a solution of vinegar and water.

PLASTIC TABLE TOPS
You will find that a coat of Turtle Wax is a quick pick-up for dulled plastic table tops and counters.

Or, rub in toothpaste and buff.

GLASS TABLE TOPS
Rub in a little lemon juice. Dry with paper towels and shine with newspaper for a sparkling table.

Toothpaste will remove small scratches from glass.

CHROME CLEANING
For sparkling clean chrome without streaks, use a cloth dampened in ammonia.

REMOVING GLUE
Cement glue can be removed by rubbing with cold cream, peanut butter or salad oil.

WICKER
Wicker needs moisture, so use a humidifier in the winter.

To prevent drying out, apply lemon oil occasionally.

Never let wicker freeze. This will cause cracking and splitting.

Wash with a solution of warm salt water to keep from turning yellow.

METAL FURNITURE
To remove rust, a good scrubbing with turpentine should accomplish this job.

VINYL UPHOLSTERY
Never oil vinyl as this will make it hard. It is almost impossible to soften again. For proper cleaning, sprinkle baking soda or vinegar on a rough, damp cloth, then wash with a mild dishwashing soap.

LEATHER UPHOLSTERY
Prevent leather from cracking by polishing regularly with a cream made of 1 part vinegar and 2 parts linseed oil. Clean with a damp cloth and saddle soap.

GREASE STAINS
Absorb grease on furniture by pouring salt on the spill immediately.

SOILED UPHOLSTERY
Rub soiled cotton upholstery fabric with an artgum eraser or squares (purchased at stationery store).

LAUNDRY

SPOT REMOVAL
Two parts water and one part rubbing alcohol are the basic ingredients in any commercial spot remover.

CLEAN MACHINE
Fill your washer with warm water and add a gallon of distilled vinegar. Run the machine through the entire cycle to unclog and clean soap scum from hoses.

TOO SUDSY
When your washer overflows with too many suds, sprinkle salt in the water - the suds will disappear.

HAND-WASHED SWEATERS
Add a capful of hair cream rinse to the final rinse water when washing sweaters.

WHITER FABRIC
Linen or cotton can be whitened by boiling in a mixture or 1 part cream of tartar and 3 parts water.

WHITEST SOCKS
Boil socks in water to which a lemon slice has been added.

FRESHEN FEATHER PILLOWS
Put feather pillows in the dryer and tumble, then air outside.

LINTLESS CORDUROY
While corduroy is still damp, brush with clothes brush to remove all lint.

IRONING TIP
When pressing pants, iron the top part on the wrong side. Iron the legs on the right side. This gives the pockets and waistband a smooth look.

CREASELESS GARMENTS
Take an empty cardboard paper towel roll and cut through it lengthwise. Slip it over a wire hanger to prevent a crease from forming in the garment to be hung on the hanger.

REMOVE CREASES FROM HEMS
Sponge material with a white vinegar solution and press flat to remove creases in hems.

BEDROOM IRONING
A good place to iron is in the bedroom. Closets are nearby to hang clothes up immediately, and the bed makes a good surface on which to fold clothes and separate items into piles.

IRONING BOARD COVER
When washing your ironing board cover, attach it to the board while it is still damp. When it dries, the surface will be completely smooth.

Starch your ironing board cover. This helps the cover stay clean longer.

LINT REMOVER
Add a yard of nylon netting to your dryer with the wet clothes - it will catch most of the lint.

WASHER ADVICE
Button all buttons on clothing and turn inside out before putting into the washer. Fewer buttons will fall off and garments will fade less if turned inside out.

SOILED COLLARS
Use a small paintbrush and brush hair shampoo into soiled shirt collars before laundering. Shampoo is made to dissolve body oils.

FASTER IRONING
Place a strip of heavy-duty aluminum foil over the entire length of the ironing board and cover with pad. As you iron, heat will reflect through the underside of the garment.

IRONING EMBROIDERY
Lay the embroidery piece upside-down on a Turkish towel before ironing. All the little spaces between the embroidery will be smooth when you are finished.

BATHROOM

BATHROOM TILE
Rub ordinary car wax into your ceramic bathroom tiling to clean and refinish. Let it stand 10 minutes and buff or polish.

Use a typewriter eraser to clean spaces between bathroom tiles.

CERAMIC TILES
Before cleaning bathroom tiles, run the shower on *Hot* for 5 minutes to steam the dirt loose.

METAL SHOWER HEAD
To clean mineral deposits from a clogged shower head, boil it with half a cup of white vinegar.

PLASTIC SHOWER HEAD
Soak a plastic shower head in a hot vinegar and water mixture to unclog it.

SHOWER CURTAINS
Before hanging shower curtains, soak them in a salt water solution to prevent mildew.

To remove mildew on shower curtains, wash them in hot soapy water, rub with lemon juice, and let them dry in the sun.

BATHROOM FIXTURES
Dip a cloth in kerosene or rubbing alcohol to remove scum from your bathroom fixtures.

REMOVING FILM AND SCUM
Use a piece of very fine steel wool to remove film from the shower stall.

PORCELAIN CLEANERS
Lighter fluid will remove most dark, stubborn stains from sink and bathtub.

YELLOWED BATHTUB
Restore whiteness to a yellowed bathtub by rubbing with a salt and turpentine solution.

TOILET
Sometimes moisture accumulates around the toilet, leaving puddles on the floor. Prevent the condensation by applying a coat of floor wax to the tank.

RUST STAINS
Spread a paste of hydrogen peroxide and cream of tartar over the area, and add a few drops of ammonia. Let it stand for 2 or 3 hours.

RUSTY TILE
Rust stains on tile can be removed with kerosene.

CLEANING SHOWER DOORS
Rub glass shower doors with a white vinegar-dampened sponge to remove soap residue.

STEAM-FREE MIRROR
If your medicine cabinet has two sliding mirrors, slide one side open before taking a bath or shower. After the bath, you'll have one clean mirror instead of two that are steamed and foggy.

STEAMY BATHROOMS
If you run about an inch of cold water before adding hot water to your bath, there will be absolutely no steam in your bathroom.

MEDICINE CABINET
It's a good idea to go through your medicine cabinet several times a year and throw away medicines that are old or outdated. They could be dangerous.

EASY BATHROOM CLEANING
Clean your bathroom after a steamy bath or shower. The walls, fixtures, etc., will be much easier to clean because the steam will have loosened the dirt.

SINK CLEANERS
Light stains can often be removed by simply rubbing with a cut lemon.

For dark stains, and especially rust, rub with a paste of borax and lemon juice.

SWEET-SMELLING BATHROOM
Place a fabric softener sheet in the wastepaper basket. Or, add a touch of fragrance by dabbing your favorite perfume on a light bulb. When the light is on, the heat releases the aroma.

HANDY PERSON

PLYWOOD CUTTING
Put a strip of masking tape at the point of plywood where you plan to begin sawing to keep it from splitting.

LOCATING WALL STUDS
Move a pocket compass along the wall. When the needle moves, usually the stud will be located at that point. Studs are usually located 16" apart.

FRAYING ROPE
Shellac the ends of the rope to prevent fraying.

Heat the cut end of the nylon cord over a match flame to bond the end together.

LOOSENING RUSTY BOLTS
Apply a cloth soaked in any carbonated soda to loosen rusted bolts.

SANDPAPER HINT
By dampening the backing on sandpaper, it will last longer and resist cracking.

TIGHT SCREWS
Loosen a screw by putting a couple of drops of peroxide on it and letting it soak in.

SCREWDRIVER TIP
Keep a screwdriver tip from slipping by putting chalk on the blade.

LOOSENING JOINTS
Loosen old glue by applying vinegar from an oil can to the joint.

RULE TO REMEMBER
Left is loose and right is tight.

STICKING DRAWERS
Rub the runners of drawers with a candle or a bar of soap so they will slide easily.

STUBBORN LOCKS
Dip key into machine oil or graphite to loosen up a lock.

LOOSE DRAWER KNOBS
Before inserting a screw into the knob, coat with fingernail polish to hold it tightly.

SLAMMING DOORS
Reduce the noise level in your home by putting self-sticking protective pads on the inside edges of cabinet doors, cupboards, etc.

ICY SIDEWALK TIP
Sprinkle sand through a strainer or an icy sidewalk to distribute evenly.

GARBAGE CAN TIP
Garbage cans will last longer if they are painted. Use primer on galvanized metal, then paint with matching house paint.

TOWEL RACK TIP
Replace the bottom screws of towel racks with cup hooks. Small towels and washcloths may be hung from them.

SCREEN REPAIR
Use clear cement glue to repair a small hole in wire screening.

HAIR DRYER HINT
Thaw a frozen pipe with a portable hairdryer.

FINDING A GAS LEAK
Lather the pipes with soapy water. The escaping gas will cause the soapy water to bubble, revealing the damaged areas. You can make a temporary plug by moistening a cake of soap and pressing it over the spot. When the soap hardens, it will effectively close the leak until the gasman comes.

HANGING PICTURES
Before you drive nails into the wall, mark the spot with an X of cellophane tape. This trick will keep the plaster from cracking when you start hammering.

When the landlady says, "no nails in the wall", hang pictures with sewing machine needles. They will hold up to 30 pounds.

BEAUTY

NATURAL FACIAL
A good and inexpensive facial to try; mash half an avocado, spread thickly on face and remove with warm water 20 minutes later.

SUNBURN RELIEF
A wonderful relief for sunburn pain is the application of mint-flavored milk of magnesia to the skin.

Dab on some apple cider vinegar. The pinkness and pain will disappear.

For a super bad burn, put on a paste of water and baking soda.

BROKEN LIPSTICK
Hold a match under the broken ends until they melt enough to adhere to each other. Cool in the refrigerator.

HAIR SHINER
These hair rinses will remove soap film and shine hair: For blondes, rinse water containing a few tablespoons of lemon juice. For brunettes and redheads, a few tablespoons of apple cider vinegar in the rinse water.

NAIL POLISH
Don't throw away that gummy nail polish. Place the bottle in boiling water to bring it back to its original consistency.

Instead of storing the nail polish bottle right-side-up, put it on its side. Stir it up with the brush when you need some.

Before you put on polish, put vinegar on your nails. It will clean them completely and help nail polish stick longer.

YOUR OWN MANICURE
Soak your hands in warm water with lemon juice added. Take them out after about 8 minutes. Rub some lemon peel over the nails while you gently push back the cuticle. Then buff with a soft cloth.

BAKING SODA FOR TEETH
Baking soda instead of toothpaste does as good a job. It also works on dentures.

CLEANING COMBS AND BRUSHES
A solution of baking soda and hot water cleans hair brushes and combs.

HAIR CONDITIONER
Mayonnaise gives dry hair a good conditioning. Apply 1/2 cup mayonnaise to dry, unwashed hair. Cover with plastic bag and wait for 15 minutes. Rinse a few times before shampooing thoroughly.

TIRED EYES
Place fresh cold cucumbers slices on your eyelids to rid them of redness and puffiness.

DRY SKIN
The best remedy is also the easiest to find: water. Drink six to eight glasses a day and eat foods high in water content, such as fruits and leafy vegetables. Use a humidifier in winter. Bathe in mildly salted water (1/2 cup of salt per bath) to rehydrate your body, then apply a cream or lotion that will act as a moisturizer.

For an easy facial, mash a banana, add a tablespoon of honey and smooth the mixture on your face. After 15 minutes, rinse with warm water.

OILY SKIN

To help normalize skin, avoid spicy foods, reduce oils and fats in your diet and drink six to eight glasses of water daily.

For a refreshing facial, fill a spray bottle with tepid water and 1 teaspoon of salt, then spray the solution on your face. Blot dry with a towel. For a quick steam, heat a wet towel in the microwave and form a tent over your face.

Here's a quick facial mask: Mix 3 tablespoons each of mineral water and FULLER'S EARTH and apply the paste to your face. After 20 minutes rinse with warm water. Or try a paste of warm water and oatmeal for 10 minutes.

PIMPLES
Here's some single-pimple camouflage: use a little green eye shadow to neutralize the redness, then cover with foundation.

PUFFINESS
If your hands are puffy, hold them over your head for a couple of minutes; repeat at least three or four times a day. Elevate swollen feet for a minimum of 15 minutes.

SEWING

THREADING NEEDLES
Apply some hair spray to your finger and to the end of the thread, stiffening it enough to be easily threaded.

SHARP MACHINE NEEDLES
Sharpen sewing machine needles by stitching through sandpaper.

BUTTONS
Coat the center of buttons with clear nail polish and they'll stay on longer.

On a four-hole button, sew through two holes at a time, knotting the thread and tying off for each set of holes.

Use dental floss or elastic thread to sew buttons on children's clothing. The buttons will take a lot of wear before falling off.

DROPPED NEEDLES AND PINS
Instead of groping around your floor for fallen needles and pins, keep a magnet in your sewing kit, simply sweep it across your rug to pick up those strays.

HEAVY SEAMS
Rub seams with a bar of soap to allow a sewing machine needle to easily pass through.

SEWING MACHINE OIL
Stitch through a blotter after oiling your sewing machine to prevent extra oil from damaging your garments.

PATTERNS
Instead of trying to fit used patterns back into their envelopes, store them in plastic bags.

Keep patterns from tearing and wrinklefree by spraying with spray starch.

SEWING ON NYLON
When repairing seams on nylon jackets or lingerie, make the job a lot simpler by placing a piece of paper underneath the section you are going to sew. Stitch through the fabric and paper. When finished, tear the paper off.

IV. FOOD STORAGE

...WHAT TO KEEP, HOW TO KEEP IT AND HOW LONG TO KEEP IT

Baking Powder: Store the airtight tins in a cool, dry place and replace every 6 months.

Baking Soda: Store in an airtight container in a cool, dry place for about 6 months.

Beans: Once a package is opened, dry beans should not be refrigerated but stored in airtight containers in a cold, dry place. They will keep for about 1 year.

Bread: A rib of celery in your bread bag will keep the bread fresh for a longer time.

Brown Sugar: Wrap in a plastic bag and store in a tightly covered container for up to 4 months.

Cakes: Putting half an apple in the cake box will keep cake moist.

Celery and lettuce: Store in refrigerator in paper bags instead of plastic. Leave the outside leaves and stalks on until ready to use.

Cheese: Wrap cheese in a vinegar-dampened cloth to keep it from drying out.

Chocolate: Store chocolate for no longer than 1 year. It should be kept in a cool, dry place with a temperature range of 60°F to 75°F. If the storage temperature exceeds 75°F, some of the cocoa butter may separate and rise to the surface, causing a whitish color to the chocolate called "bloom".

Cocoa: Store cocoa in a glass jar in a dry and cool place.

Cookies: Place crushed tissue paper on the bottom your cookie jar.

Cottage cheese: Store carton upside-down. It will keep twice as long.

Dried Fruit: Store unopened packages of dried fruit in a cool, dry place or in the refrigerator. Store opened packages in an airtight container in the refrigerator or freezer for 6 to 8 months.

Flour: Store flour in a clean, tightly covered container for up to 1 year at room temperature.

Granulated Sugar: Store sugar in a tightly covered container for up to 2 years.

Garlic: Garlic should be stored in a dry, airy place away from light. Garlic cloves can be kept in the freezer. When ready to use, peel and chop before thawing. Or, garlic cloves will never dry out if you store them in a bottle of cooking oil. After the garlic is used up, you can use the garlic flavored oil for salad dressing.

Honey: Put honey in small plastic freezer containers to prevent sugaring. It also thaws out in a short time.

Ice Cream: Ice cream that has been opened and returned to the freezer sometimes forms a waxlike film on the top. To prevent this, after part of the ice cream has been removed press a piece of waxed paper against the surface and reseal the carton.

Lemons: Store whole lemons in a tightly sealed jar of water in the refrigerator. They will yield much more juice than when first purchased.

Limes: Store limes, wrapped in tissue paper, on lower shelf of the refrigerator.

Marshmallows: They will not dry out if stored in the freezer. Simply cut with scissors when ready to use.

Nuts: For optimum freshness and shelf life, nuts should be stored, preferably unshelled, in a tightly covered container in the refrigerator or freezer and shelled as needed. (The shell and the cool temperature keep the nut from turning rancid.)

Olive oil: You can lengthen the life of olive oil by adding a cube of sugar to the bottle.

Onions: Wrap individually in foil to keep them from becoming soft or sprouting. Once an onion has been cut in half, rub the leftover side with butter and it will keep fresh longer.

Parsley: Keep fresh and crisp by storing in a wide-mouth jar with a tight lid. Parsley may also be frozen.

Popcorn: It should always be kept in the freezer. Not only will it stay fresh, but freezing helps eliminate "old-maids".

Potatoes: Potatoes, as well as other root vegetables, keep well in a dark, cool place, preferably a cellar. Store them in a dark brown paper bag.

Shredded Coconut: Store in a cool, dry place in an airtight container. Do not store in the refrigerator.

Smoked meats: Wrap ham or bacon in a vinegar-soaked cloth, then in waxed paper to preserve freshness.

Soda crackers: Wrap tightly and store in the refrigerator.

Strawberries: Keep in a colander in the refrigerator. Wash just before serving.

Vegetables with tops: Remove the tops on carrots, beets, etc. before storing.

Yeast: Store in the freezer or refrigerator in a closed plastic bag.

MEAT

BEEF

Roasts	3 to 5 days
Steaks	3 to 5 days
Ground beef, stew meat	2 days

PORK

Roasts	3 to 5 days
Hams, picnics, whole	7 days
Bacon	7 to 14 days
Chops, spareribs	2 to 3 days
Pork sausage	1 to 2 days

VEAL

Roasts	3 to 5 days
Chops	4 days

LAMB

Roasts	3 to 5days
Chops	3 to 5 days
Ground amb	2 days

POULTRY

Chickens, whole	1 to 2 days
Chickens, cut up	2 days
Turkeys, whole	1 to 2 days

COOKED MEATS

Leftover cooked meats	4 days
Cooked poulty	2 days
Hams, picnics	7 days
Frankfurters	4 to 5 days
Sliced luncheon meats	3 days

V. TO REMOVE STAINS FROM WASHABLES

ALCOHOLIC BEVERAGES
Pre-soak or sponge fresh stains immediately with cold water, then with cold water and glycerin. Rinse with vinegar for a few seconds if stain remains. These stains may turn brown with age. If wine stain remains, rub with concentrated detergent; wait 15 minutes; rinse. Repeat if necessary. Wash with detergent in hottest water safe for fabric.

BABY FOOD
Use liquid laundry detergent and brush into stain with an old toothbrush then wash.

BLOOD
Pre-soak in cold or warm water at least 30 minutes. If stain remains, soak in lukewarm ammonia water (3 tablespoons per gallon water). Rinse. If stain remains, work in detergent, and wash, using bleach safe for fabric.

CANDLE WAX
Use a dull knife to scrape off as much as possible. Place fabric between 2 blotters or facial tissues and press with warm iron.

Remove color stain with non-flammable dry cleaning solvent. Wash with detergent in the hottest water safe for fabric.

CHEWING GUM
Rub area with ice, then scrape off with a dull blade. Sponge with dry cleaning solvent; allow to air dry. Wash in detergent and hottest water safe for fabric.

CHOCOLATE AND COCOA
Sponge with club soda.

COFFEE
Sponge or soak with cold water as soon as possible. Wash, using detergent and bleach safe for fabric. Remove cream grease stains with non-flammable dry cleaning solvent. Wash again.

COSMETICS
Loosen stain with a non-flammable dry cleaning solvent. Rub detergent in until stain outline is gone. Wash in hottest water and detergent safe for fabric.

CRAYON
Scrape with dull blade. Place item between paper towels, press with warm iron. Repeat, only with new paper towels. Wash in hottest water safe for fabric, with detergent and 1 to 2 cups of baking soda. NOTE: If full load is crayon stained, take to cleaners or coin-op dry cleaning machines.

DEODORANTS
Sponge area with white vinegar. If stain remains, soak with denatured alcohol. Wash with detergent in hottest water safe for fabric.

DYE
If dye transfers from a non-colorfast item during washing, immediately bleach discolored items. Repeat as necessary BEFORE drying. On whites use color remover. CAUTION: Do not use color remover in washer, or around washer and dryer as it may damage the finish.

EGG
Scrape with dull blade. Pre-soak in cold or warm water for at least 30 minutes. Remove grease with dry cleaning solvent. Wash in hottest water safe for fabric, with detergent.

FRUIT AND FRUIT JUICES
Sponge with cold water. Pre-soak in cold or warm water for at least 30 minutes. Wash with detergent and bleach safe for fabric.

GRASS
Pre-soak in cold water for at least 30 minutes. Rinse. Pre-treat with detergent, hot water, and bleach safe for fabric. On acetate and colored fabrics, use 1 part of alcohol to 2 parts water.

GREASE, OIL, TAR OR BUTTER
Method 1: Use powder or chalk absorbents to remove as much grease as possible. Pre-treat with detergent or non-flammable dry cleaning solvent, or liquid shampoo. Wash in hottest water safe for fabric, using plenty of detergent.

Method 2: Rub spot with lard and sponge with a non-flammable dry cleaning solvent. Wash in hottest water and detergent safe for fabric.

INK-BALL-POINT PEN
Spray with hair spray and launder.

KETCHUP OR MUSTARD
Scrape excess. Use commercial spot remover. Rinse; launder.

LIQUOR
Sponge stain with cool water. Soak in solution of cool water and dishwashing liquid: 30 minutes for light-stain, overnight for heavy. Rinse; launder.

MEAT JUICES
Scrape with dull blade. Pre-soak in cold or warm water for 30 minutes. Wash with detergent and bleach safe for fabric.

MILDEW
Pre-treat as soon as possible with detergent. Wash. If any stain remains, sponge with lemon juice and salt. Dry in sun. Wash, using hottest water, detergent and bleach safe for fabric.

NOTE: Mildew is very hard to remove; treat promptly.

MILK, CREAM, ICE CREAM
Pre-soak in cold or warm water for 30 minutes. Wash. Sponge any grease spots with non-flammable dry cleaning solvent. Wash again.

MUD
Let stain dry. Brush off; launder. Tough stain: Soak in cool water for 30 minutes; work liquid laundry detergent into stain; rinse.

NAIL POLISH
Sponge with acetone-based polish remover or banana oil. Wash. If stain remains, sponge with denatured alcohol to which a few drops of ammonia have been added. Wash again. Do not use polish remover on acetate or triacetate fabrics.

PAINT
Oil base: Sponge stains with turpentine, cleaning fluid or paint remover. Pre-treat and wash in hot water. For old stains, sponge with banana oil and then with non-flammable dry cleaning solvent. Wash again.

Water base: Scrape off paint with dull blade. Wash with detergent in water as hot as is safe for fabric.

PERSPIRATION
Sponge fresh stain with ammonia; old stain with vinegar. Pre-soak in cold or warm water. Rinse. Wash in hottest water safe for fabric. If fabric is yellowed, use bleach. If stain still remains, dampen and sprinkle with meat tenderizer, or pepsin. Let stand 1 hour. Brush off and wash. For persistent odor, sponge with colorless mouthwash.

RUST

Soak in lemon juice and salt or axolic acid solution (3 tablespoons oxalic acid to 1 pint warm water). A commercial rust remover may be used. CAUTION: HANDLE POISONOUS RUST REMOVERS CAREFULLY. KEEP OUT OF REACH OF CHILDREN. NEVER USE OXALIC ACID OR ANY RUST REMOVER AROUND WASHER OR DRYER AS IT CAN DAMAGE THE FINISH. SUCH CHEMICALS MAY ALSO REMOVE PERMANENT PRESS FABRIC FINISHES.

SCORCH

Wash with detergent and bleach safe for fabric. On heavier scorching, cover stain with cloth dampened with hydrogen peroxide. Cover this with dry cloth and press with hot iron. Rinse well. CAUTION: Severe scorching cannot be removed because of fabric damage.

SOFT DRINKS
Sponge immediately with cold water and alcohol. Heat and detergent may set stain.

TEA
Sponge or soak with cold water as soon as possible. Wash using detergent and bleach safe for fabric.

STAINS ON CARPETS AND FLOORS

FLATTEN SHAG CARPETS
Raise flattened spots in your carpet where heavy furniture has stood by using a steam iron. Hold the iron over the spot and build up a good steam. Then brush up the carpet.

CANDLE DRIPPINGS
For spilled wax on carpet, use a brown paper bag as a blotter and run a hot iron over it, which will absorb the wax.

DOG STAINS
Blot up excess moisture with paper towel. Pour club soda on the spot and continue blotting. Lay a towel over the spot and set a heavy object on top in order to absorb all the moisture.

RUG CARE
When washing and drying foam-backed throw rugs, never wash in hot water, and use the "air only" dryer setting to dry. Heat will ruin foam.

CLEANING RUGS
If the rug is only slightly dirty, you can clean it with cornmeal. Use a stiff brush to work the cornmeal into the pile of the rug. Take it all out with the vacuum.

SPILLS ON THE RUG
When spills happen, go to the bathroom and grab a can of shaving cream. Squirt it on the spot then rinse off with water.

BALLPOINT INK MARKS
Saturate the spots with hairspray. Allow to dry. Brush lightly with a solution of water and vinegar.

GLUE
Glue can be loosened by saturating the spot with a cloth soaked in vinegar.

REPAIRING BRAIDED RUGS
Braided rugs often rip apart. Instead of sewing them, use clear fabric glue to repair. It's that fast and easy.

REPAIRING A BURN
Remove some fuzz from the carpet, either by shaving or pulling out with a tweezer. Roll into the shape of the burn. Apply a good cement glue to the backing of the rug and press the fuzz down into the burned spot. Cover with a piece of cleansing tissue and place a heavy book on top. This will cause the glue to dry very slowly and will get the best results.

SPOT REMOVER FOR OUTDOOR CARPETING
Spray spots liberally with a pre-wash commercial spray. Let it set several minutes, then hose down and watch the spots disappear.

BLOOD ON THE RUG
When you get blood on your rug, rub off as much as you can at first, then take a cloth soaked in cold water and wet the spot, wiping it up as you go. If a little bit remains, pour some ammonia onto the cool, wet cloth and lightly wipe that over the spot, too. Rinse it right away with cold water.

CRAYON MARKS
Use silver polish to remove from vinyl tile or linoleum.

SPILLED NAIL POLISH
Allow to almost dry, then peel off of waxed floors or tile.

TAR SPOTS
Use paste wax to remove tar from floors. Works on shoes, too.

DUSTING FLOORS
Stretch a nylon stocking over the dust mop. After using, discard the stocking and you will have a clean mop.

VARNISHED FLOORS
Use cold tea to clean woodwork and varnished floors.

SPILLED GREASE
Rub floor with ice cubes to solidify grease. Scrape up excess and wash with soapy water.

QUICK SHINE
Put a piece of waxed paper under your dust mop. Dirt will stick to the mop and the wax will shine your floors.

UNMARRED FLOORS
Put thick old socks over the legs of heavy furniture when moving across floors.

WOOD FLOOR CARE
Never use water or water-based cleaners on wood floors. Over a period of time, warping and swelling will develop.

FLOOR POLISHER
When cleaning the felt pads of your floor polisher, place the pads between layers of newspaper and press with an iron to absorb built-up wax.

GARAGE FLOORS
In an area where a large amount of oil has spilled, lay several thicknesses of newspaper. Saturate the paper with water; press flat against the floor. When dry, remove the newspaper and the spots will have disappeared.

BASEMENT FLOORS
Sprinkle sand on oily spots, let it absorb the oil, and sweep up.

FIX THOSE LOOSE LINOLEUM EDGES
Take a knife with some tile adhesive and work it under the loose part. Put a heavy weight, such as a big stack of books, over the whole area and keep it weighed down for the amount of time it says on the can of adhesive.

HEEL MARKS
Just take a pencil eraser and wipe them off.

VI. 99 WAYS YOU CAN SAVE THE EARTH

1. Buy plain white toilet paper, tissues and paper towels. Dyed paper pollutes.

2. Instead of ammonia-based cleaners, use vinegar and water or baking soda and water.

3. Walk or ride a bike instead of using the car for short trips.

4. Reuse your grocery bags, or buy a string bag you can carry your groceries in.

5. Buy eggs and milk in cardboard cartons instead of plastic. Or recycle your plastic milk jugs.

6. Take showers instead of baths to save water and energy.

7. Keep your car tires inflated to the proper pressure to improve fuel economy and extend the life of the tires.

8. Don't use electric tools and appliances when hand-operated ones will do the job.

9. Choose a light-colored car with tinted glass to lessen the need for air conditioning.

10. Use mulch and natural ground covers in gardens to contain moisture and conserve water use.

11. Instead of ironing, hang clothes in the bathroom while you shower.

12. Turn off lights in rooms you aren't using.

13. Replace incandescent bulbs with more efficient screw-in compact fluorescent bulbs or fluorescent fixtures.

14. Use high-quality multigrade oil in your car to increase fuel efficiency.

15. Air-dry laundry when possible.

16. Avoid keeping refrigerator or freezer too cold. Government recommended temperature for fresh food is 38 degrees F. For freezers it's 5 degrees F.

17. Reuse aluminum foil and plastic wrap, or avoid them completely by using plastic containers.

18. Plant trees. Strategically located, trees can reduce heating and cooling bills, help prevent soil erosion and reduce air pollution.

19. Water lawns at night to limit evaporation.

20. Compost your leaves and yard waste. You'll improve your garden's soil and avoid sending yard waste to the landfill.

21. Minimize the use of garden chemicals by weeding.

22. Be sure to return your recyclable cans and bottles for your deposit.

23. Don't pour oil and gasoline into the sewer system or on the ground. Take to your local collection site.

24. Buy rechargeable batteries.

25. Use cold water rather than hot water whenever possible for kitchen tasks and laundry.

26. Share rides to work or use public transportation.

27. Buy a fuel-efficient car. Aim for 35 miles per gallon.

28. Read labels and research the products you buy.

29. Don't use excessive amounts of detergent. Presoak dirty laundry.

30. Insulate your basement to save 1/3 on your heat bill.

31. Buy products packaged in recycled paper or cardboard.

32. Caulk and weatherstrip doors and windows.

33. Ask your utility company for an energy audit to assess energy waste in your home.

34. Install water-conserving showerheads and sink-faucet aerators.

35. Insulate your water heater. Turn it down to 121 degrees F.

36. Limit or eliminate your use of "disposable" items.

37. Close off unused areas of your home. Shut off or block heat vents.

38. Compare Energy Guide labels when buying appliances.

39. Keep the fireplace damper closed to prevent heat escape. Keep glass fireplace doors closed when a fire is burning.

40. Use an automatic setback thermostat to turn down heat when you're not home and at night.

41. Capture free solar heat in the winter by opening curtains on south windows during sunny days.

42. Clean lamps and lighting fixtures regularly.

43. Thaw frozen foods in the refrigerator to reduce cooking times and to ensure food safety.

44. Tune up your car regularly for maximum gas mileage.

45. Remove unnecessary items from your car. Each 100 pounds of weight decreases fuel efficiency by 1%.

46. Don't speed; accelerate and slow down gradually.

47. Use latex and other water-based paints instead of toxic enamel or oil-based paints.

48. Repair leaks and drips as soon as they occur. A moderate drip wastes two gallons of water or more per hour.

49. Rent or borrow items you don't often use. Efficient use of products conserves resources.

50. Use small electric pans and ovens to reduce energy use.

51. Run your dishwasher only when full, and use the energy saver cycle.

52. Avoid products made from tropical rainforest woods.

53. Request a Household Hazardous Waste Wheel, showing alternatives to hazardous products, from the Department of Natural Resources, 1-800-DNR-1025 (cost $1.25).

54. For furniture polish, use 1 part lemon juice, 2 parts olive or vegetable oil.

55. For a toilet bowl cleaner, use baking soda and a brush.

56. As a general cleaner, use 1/2 cup borax in 1 gallon water.

57. Instead of chemical air fresheners, set a cotton ball soaked in vanilla extract on a saucer. (Keep away from children and pets.)

58. Instead of toxic mothballs, use cedar chips.

59. Roach killer: Mix baking soda and powdered sugar. (Keep away from children and pets.)

60. Ant killer: Use chili powder to hinder entry.

61. Do not toss toxic chemicals into your garbage. Call the Ground-water Hotline 1-800-DNR-1025 to find out how to dispose, or keep them for a Toxic Cleanup Day.

62. Use pump sprays instead of aerosols.

63. Use a holding tank on your boat and don't empty toilet tanks into the water.

64. Don't litter. Pick up any you see, especially plastic rings that can trap birds and fish.

65. Take your own coffee cup to work instead of using disposables.

66. Pour a kettle of boiling water down the drain weekly to melt fat that may be building up.

67. Take old tires to a landfill or processing center for proper disposal.

68. Buy recycled paper, stationery and greeting cards.

69. Shop at your local farmers market. Products are fresh, packaging is minimal and foods are less likely to be made with preservatives.

70. Start an organic garden.

71. Buy in bulk to avoid over packaging.

72. Avoid optional equipment on cars that decreases fuel economy.

73. When having air conditioners serviced, choose companies that will recycle freon instead of venting it.

74. Keep lint screen in dryer clean.

75. Use a trash bag in your car instead of throwing trash out the window.

76. Consider using cloth diapers instead of disposable ones. Check for a local diaper service.

77. Urge your local community to start a curbside recycling program.

78. Start a recycling program where you work. Contact the Department of Natural Resources about the Waste Reduction Assistance Program (WRAP) at 1-800-DNR-1025.

79. Insulate your waterbed by adding an inch of polyethylene foam around the edges and the bottom.

80. To remove rust, rub rust spots briskly with a piece of crumpled aluminum foil, shiny side up.

81. Give leftover paint to theater groups, schools or church groups.

82. Call your local humane society to see if they can use your old newspapers for animal bedding.

83. Check your smoke detector. Put a new battery in if it needs one. Some detectors contain small amounts of low-level radioactive waste. Send used or broken detectors back to the manufacturer.

84. Use equal parts white vinegar and warm water to wash windows or glass. Dry with a soft cloth.

85. Install storm windows.

86. When using hazardous products, use only what is needed. Twice as much does not mean twice the results.

87. Arrange for a waste management presentation for your club or business.

88. Read publications that educate about long-term sustainability.

89. Educate your children about the environment.

90. Write a letter to the editor about your environmental concerns.

91. Get involved in a local treeplanting effort.

92. Learn about global climate change.

93. Join an environmental organization.

94. Research environmental legislation and write to your representatives in the state legislature and in Congress.

95. Think about the kind of Earth you would like to see for your grandchildren's grandchildren.

96. Plan an environmental activity for your club or troop, such as a recycling program.

97. Investigate the environmental record of companies you invest in. Write a letter as a shareholder to the company president or sell your stock.

98. Talk to friends, relatives and co-workers about the environment.

99. Copy this list and send it to your friends.

VII. PLANTS

Always choose a pot that's not more than two inches larger in diameter than the old pot.

Blooming plants should be repotted after they're done blossoming, not before.

To help reduce the shock of repotting, give the new soil a thorough watering.

Clay pots should be soaked in water for a few minutes before you repot your plants. This prevents the clay from absorbing moisture from the potting soil.

Fill a string mesh bag with suet and scraps of leftover food and hang from a tree limb for those cheery winter birds.

After holidays—remove branches from Christmas tree and put them over flower beds for insulation.

Take old Christmas tree outside and stabilize in the ground. Hang grapefruit and orange cups from the branches with wire and fill cups with bird seed for the birdies.

When you start seeds indoors, it's best to plant them in a small amount of dirt at first. Gradually add more dirt as the plant grows. Do this and your plants will be much stronger and do better after you set them outside.

If you have a large garden, but not a lot of time to weed, put two layers of newspaper between your rows. This keeps the weeds down and saves you a lot of time.

Plant pole beans next to sunflowers. The beans will climb the lower part of the sunflowers and you won't need any poles.

Your African Violets will bloom longer, prettier and more abundantly if you stick a few rusty nails in the soil alongside them.